MATHS TODAY

BOOK 1

Addition

Subtraction

Multiplication

Division

Length

Fractions

Time

Money

Shape

Graphs

Addition

6 + 3 = ☐
7 + 2 = ☐
5 + 4 = ☐

3 + 4 = ☐
1 + 6 = ☐
2 + 5 = ☐

5 + 3 = ☐
4 + 4 = ☐
6 + 2 = ☐

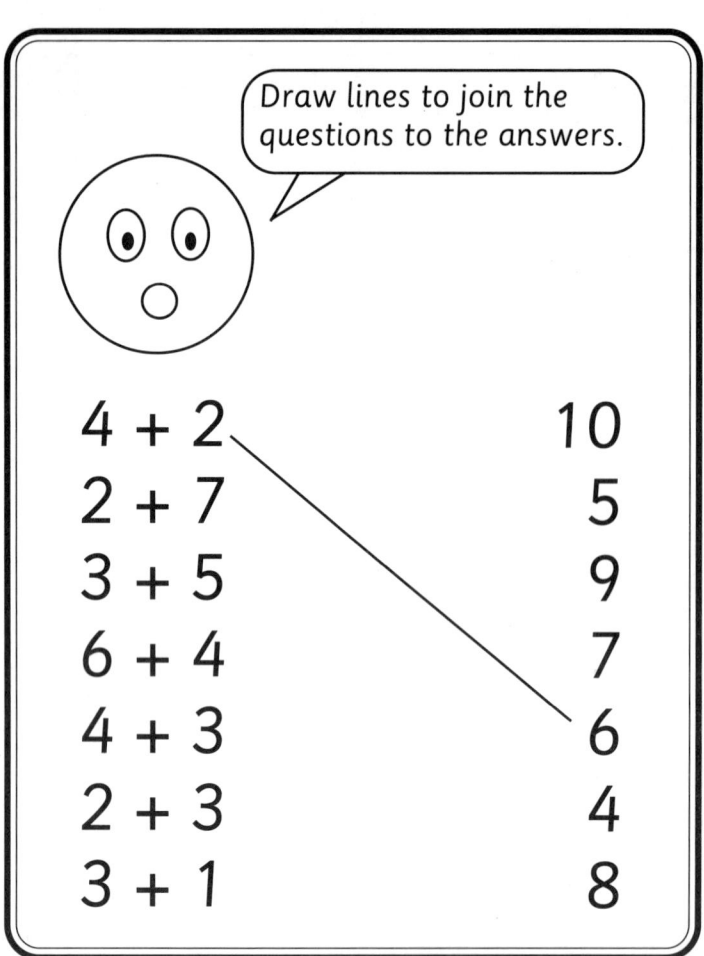

Draw lines to join the questions to the answers.

4 + 2   10
2 + 7   5
3 + 5   9
6 + 4   7
4 + 3   6
2 + 3   4
3 + 1   8

Find some ways to make ten.

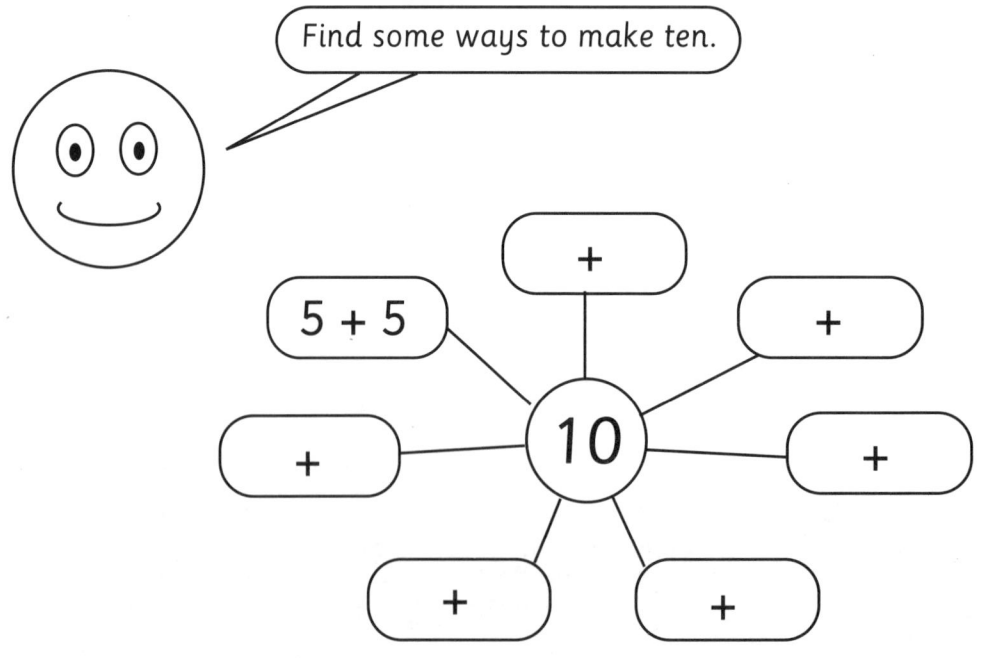

5 + 5

Making 12

We can add numbers together to make 12 in lots of ways.

12

6 + 6 = 12

11 + 1 = 12   1 + 11 = 12
10 + 2 = 12   2 + 10 = 12
9 + 3 = 12   3 + 9 = 12
8 + 4 = 12   4 + 8 = 12
7 + 5 = 12   5 + 7 = 12

See how many ways you can make 11.

11

10 + 1 = 11   ☐ + ☐ = 11
9 + 2 = 11   ☐ + ☐ = 11
8 + 3 = 11   ☐ + ☐ = 11
7 + 4 = 11   ☐ + ☐ = 11
6 + 5 = 11   ☐ + ☐ = 11

Number Speed

Try to answer these questions as quickly as possible.

0 + 3 =

4 + 2 =

7 + 1 =

5 + 4 =

6 + 2 =

1 + 5 =

3 + 7 =

6 + 3 =

5 + 2 =

3 + 3 =

4 + 3 =

7 + 0 =

2 + 4 =

0 + 8 =

4 + 4 =

8 + 2 =

3

Subtraction

10 - 6 = ☐
10 - 8 = ☐
10 - 4 = ☐

8 - 3 = ☐
8 - 5 = ☐
8 - 2 = ☐

12 - 6 = ☐
12 - 4 = ☐
12 - 9 = ☐

Draw lines to join the questions to the answers.

12 - 7   3
9 - 6   4
11 - 5   1
8 - 4   12
7 - 5   5
10 - 9   2
12 - 0   6

Try these subtractions from 9.

9 - 9 = ☐   9 - 8 = ☐
9 - 7 = ☐   9 - 6 = ☐
9 - 5 = ☐   9 - 4 = ☐
9 - 3 = ☐   9 - 2 = ☐
9 - 1 = ☐   9 - 0 = ☐

Count the stars and the circles.

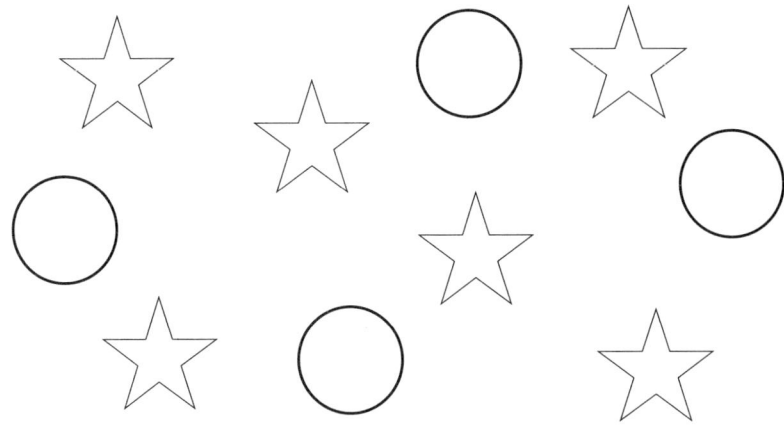

How many stars are there?

There are ☐ stars.

How many circles are there?

There are ☐ circles.

How many more stars than circles are there?

There are ☐ more stars than circles.

There are ☐ stars and circles altogether.

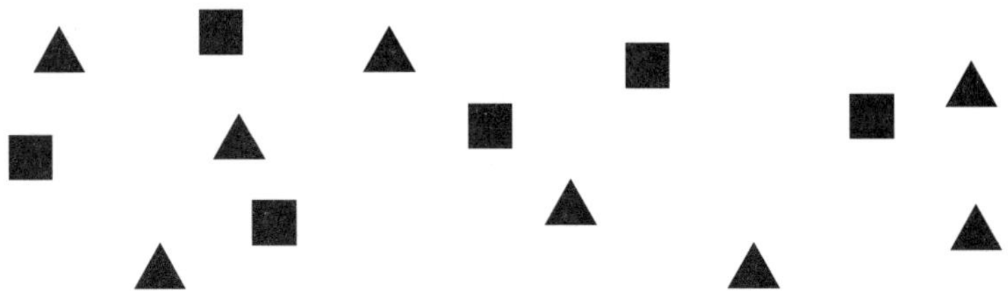

How many more triangles than squares are there?

There are ☐ more triangles than squares.

Number Speed

Try to answer these questions as quickly as possible.

6 - 2 =

4 - 3 =

8 - 5 =

12 - 7 =

9 - 4 =

10 - 5 =

7 - 6 =

5 - 3 =

11 - 9 =

8 - 8 =

6 - 0 =

12 - 4 =

10 - 6 =

7 - 3 =

4 - 2 =

9 - 8 =

Time

What times are shown on the clocks?

4 o'clock

Match the clocks to the correct times.

Number Speed

Try to answer these questions as quickly as possible.

3 + 4 =

5 - 2 =

6 + 6 =

9 - 3 =

5 + 7 =

8 - 3 =

4 + 6 =

11 - 5 =

7 + 4 =

9 - 6 =

4 + 4 =

12 - 8 =

3 + 3 =

4 - 2 =

3 + 7 =

10 - 7 =

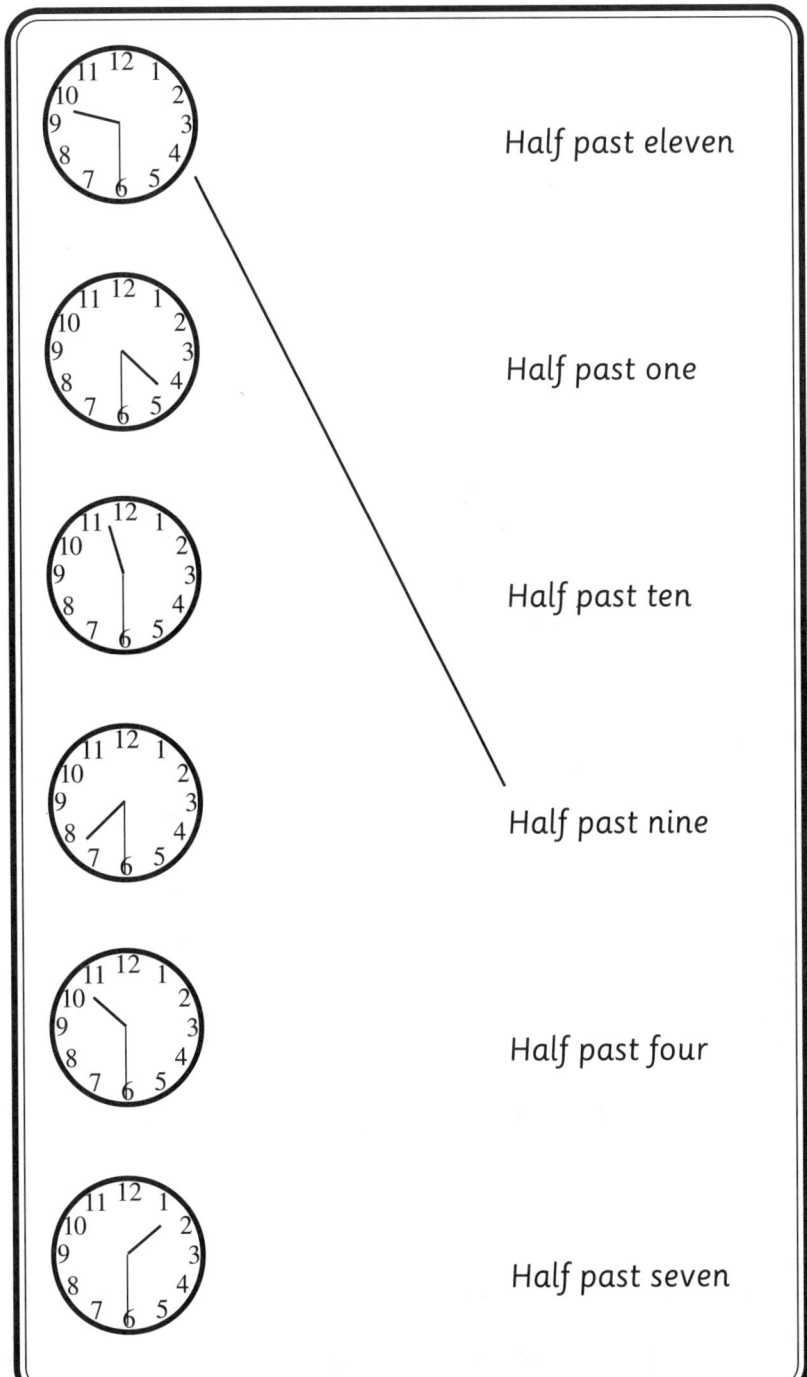

Half past eleven

Half past one

Half past ten

Half past nine

Half past four

Half past seven

Money

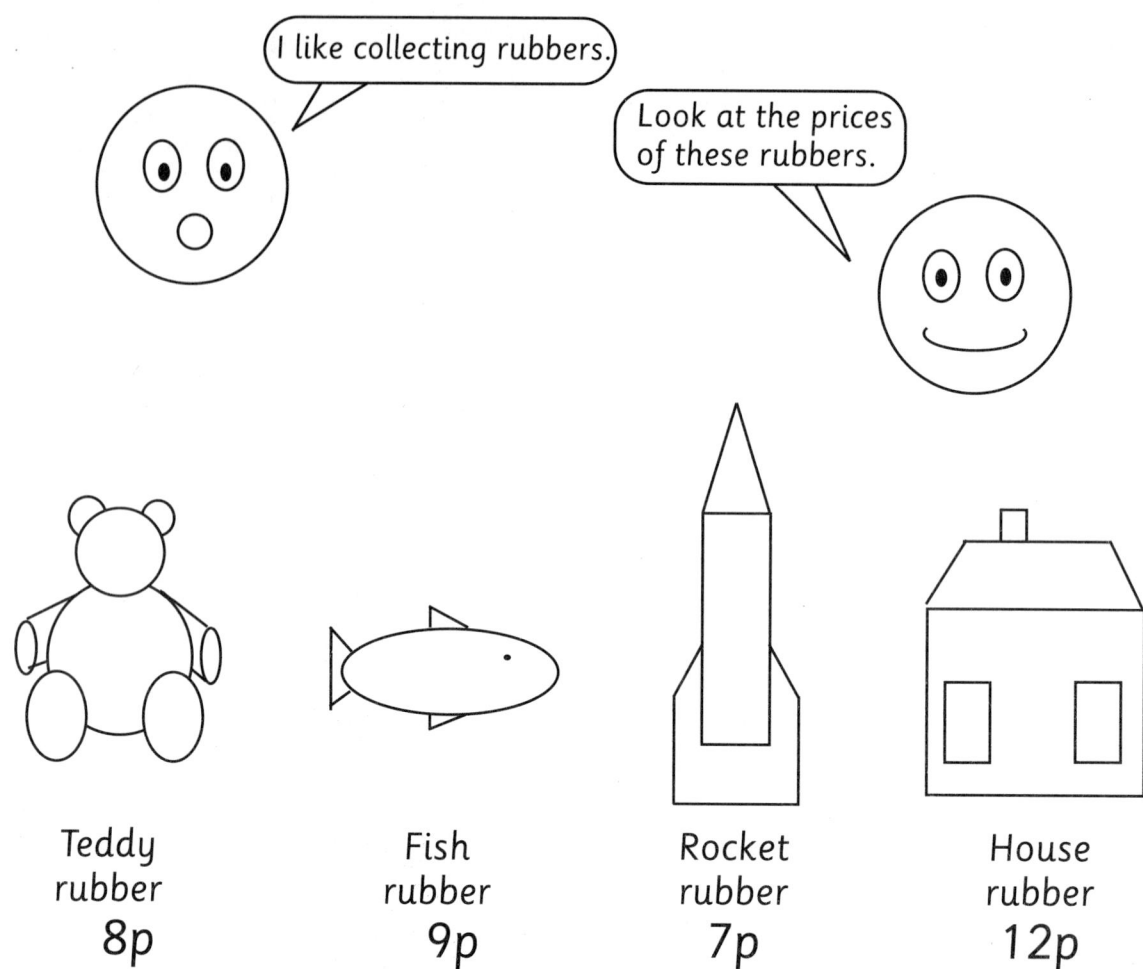

Which rubber is most expensive? _____

Which rubber is cheapest? _____

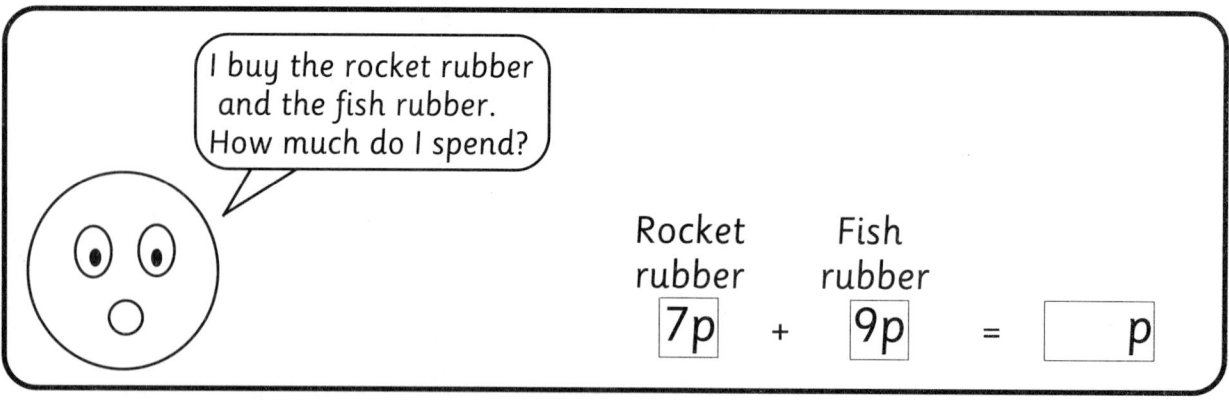

 I would like to buy three rubbers.

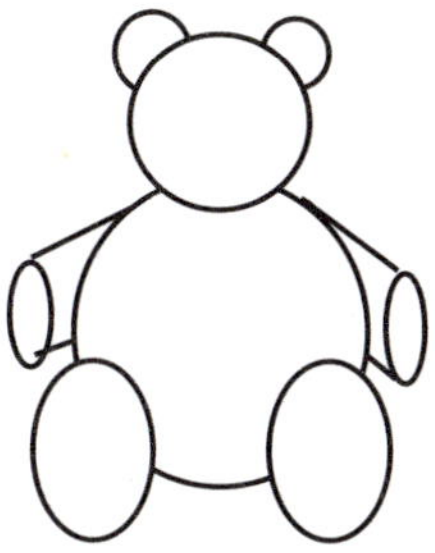

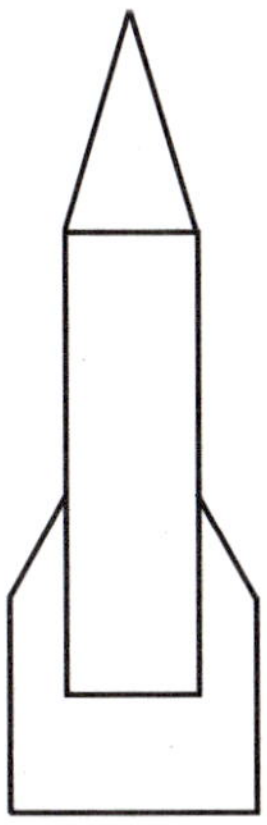

Fish rubber 9p

Teddy rubber 8p

Rocket rubber 7p

 How much do the three rubbers cost altogether?

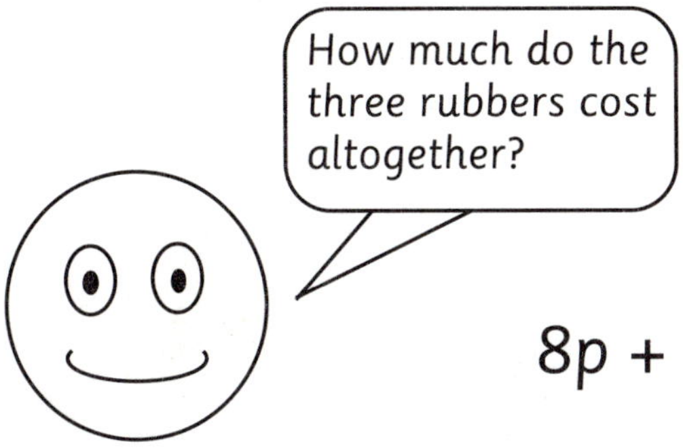

8p + 7p + 9p = 24p

Try these money additions:

6p + 2p + 3p = ☐ p
5p + 3p + 2p = ☐ p
2p + 5p + 2p =
1p + 6p + 3p =
4p + 3p + 2p =

Number Speed

Try to answer these questions as quickly as possible.

6 + 7 =

8 + 9 =

7 + 4 =

8 + 6 =

9 + 5 =

8 + 8 =

10 + 7 =

7 + 9 =

12 + 8 =

11 + 6 =

9 + 9 =

4 + 12 =

10 + 8 =

7 + 12 =

6 + 5 =

8 + 7 =

More money

7p - 4p = ☐ p
8p - 3p = ☐ p
10p - 6p = ☐ p
8p - 7p = ☐ p
14p - 6p = ☐ p

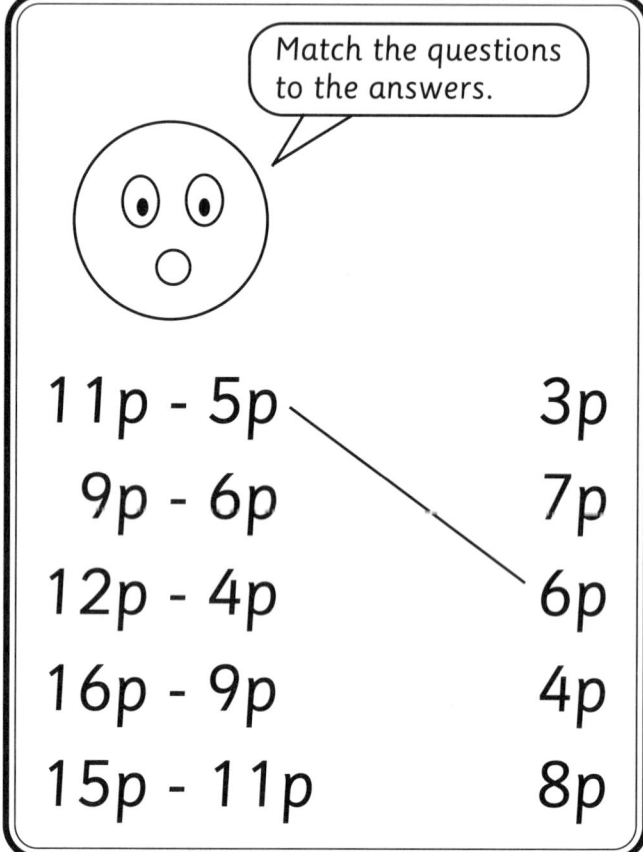

Take away from 10p.

10p - 6p = ☐ p   10p - 6p = ☐ p
10p - 5p = ☐ p   10p - 5p = ☐ p
10p - 7p = ☐ p   10p - 7p = ☐ p

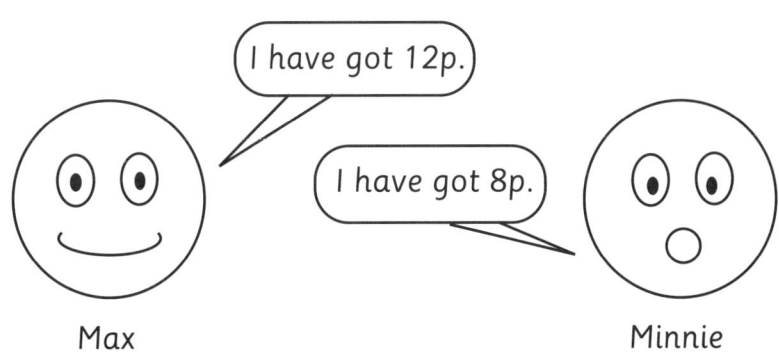

Max has got 12p.
Minnie has got 8p.

How much money have Max and Minnie got altogether? p

How much more money has Max than Minnie? p

How much will two teddy rubbers cost? p

How much will three teddy rubbers cost? p

Number Speed

Try to answer these questions as quickly as possible.

8 - 4 =

10 - 7 =

12 - 6 =

15 - 9 =

7 - 3 =

9 - 4 =

14 - 8 =

17 - 6 =

20 - 10 =

20 - 12 =

11 - 5 =

6 - 4 =

20 - 8 =

15 - 6 =

9 - 5 =

19 - 10 =

17 - 9 =

Missing numbers

What number comes next?

1) 1, 2, 3, 4, 5, ☐
2) 9, 10, 11, 12, ☐
3) 11, 12, 13, 14, ☐
4) 14, 15, 16, 17, ☐

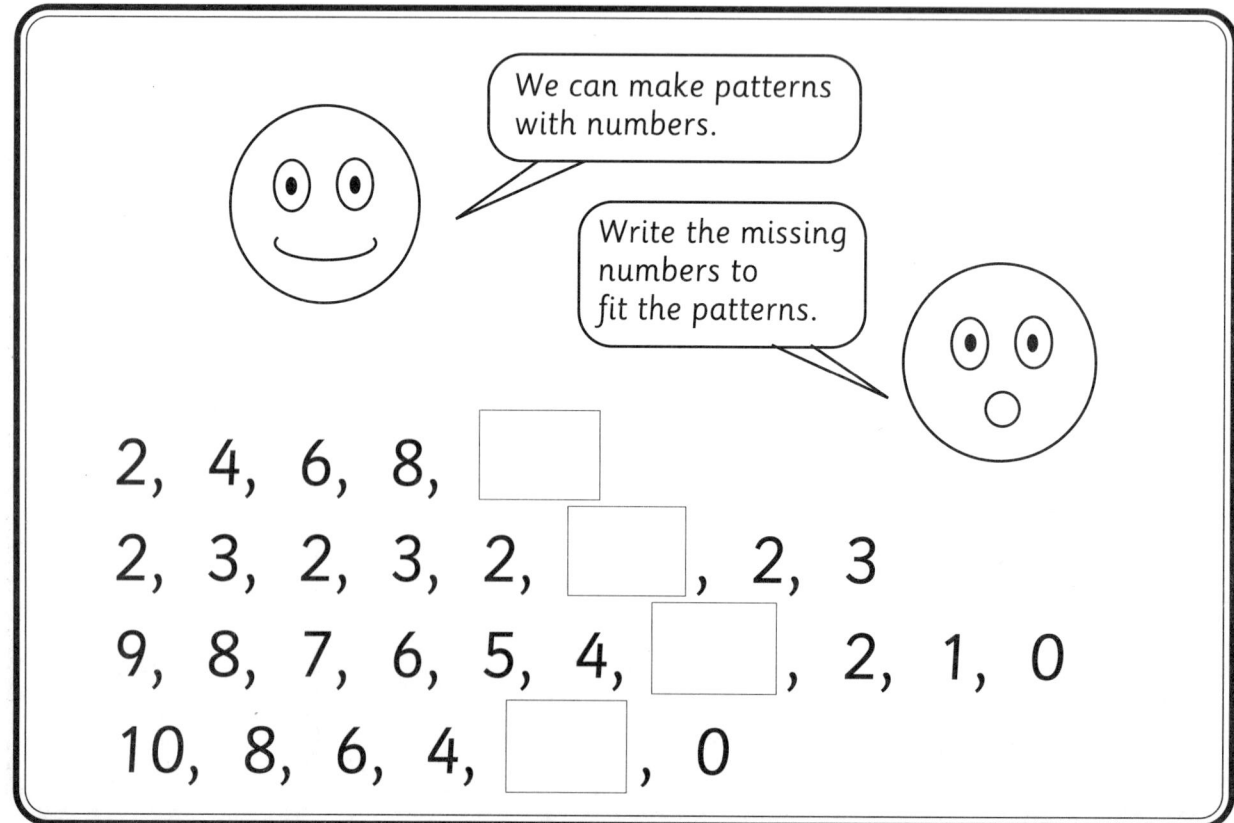

We can make patterns with numbers.

Write the missing numbers to fit the patterns.

2, 4, 6, 8, ☐

2, 3, 2, 3, 2, ☐, 2, 3

9, 8, 7, 6, 5, 4, ☐, 2, 1, 0

10, 8, 6, 4, ☐, 0

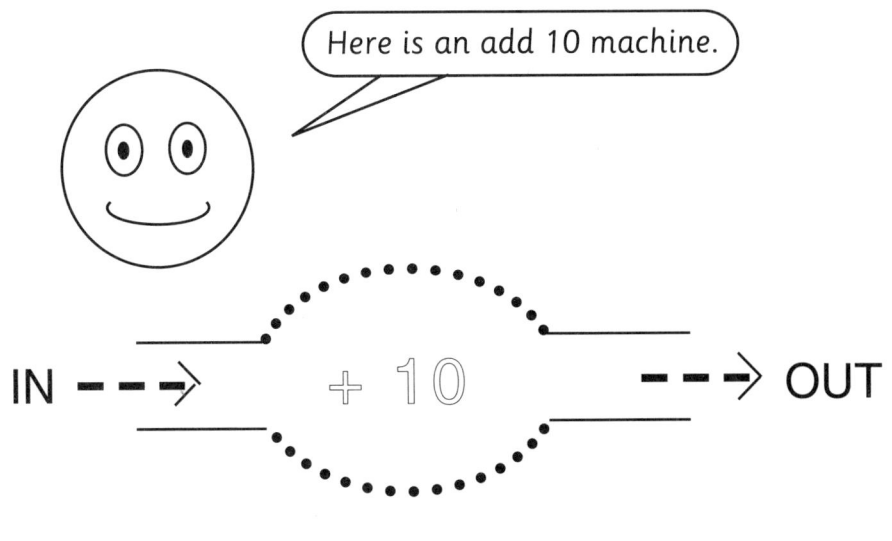

Here is an add 10 machine.

IN ---> + 10 ---> OUT

10 is added to every number which goes in.

Fill in the chart for the add 10 machine:

IN ---> + 10 ---> OUT

In	Out
6	16
4	
7	
10	
3	
20	
16	

Number Speed

Try to answer these questions as quickly as possible.

10 + 10 =

20 + 10 =

30 + 20 =

30 - 10 =

40 - 20 =

50 + 10 =

50 - 40 =

70 - 10 =

60 - 30 =

12 + 10 =

21 + 10 =

32 + 10 =

10 + 17 =

26 + 10 =

10 + 19 =

10 + 23 =

46 + 10 =

Subtraction machines

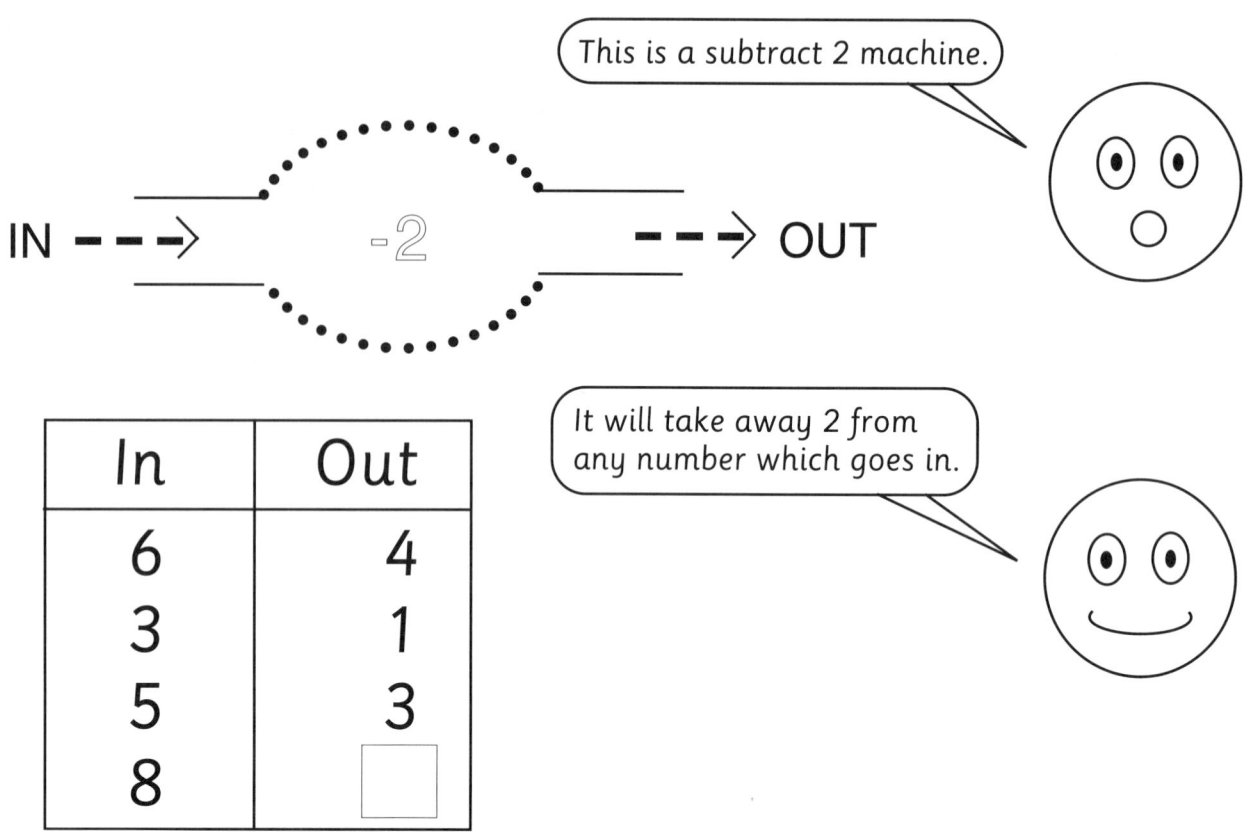

Fill in the answers for these machines:

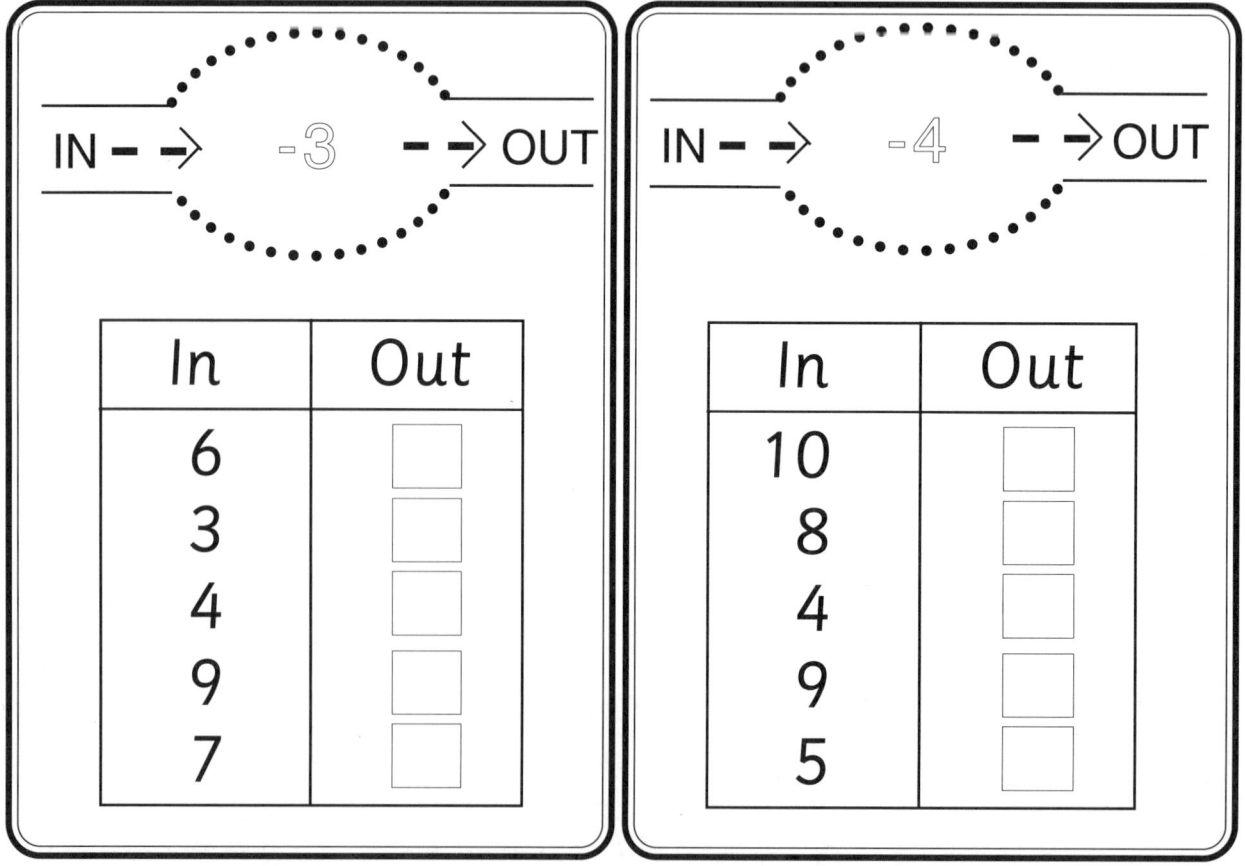

Max and Minnie played a game of darts.

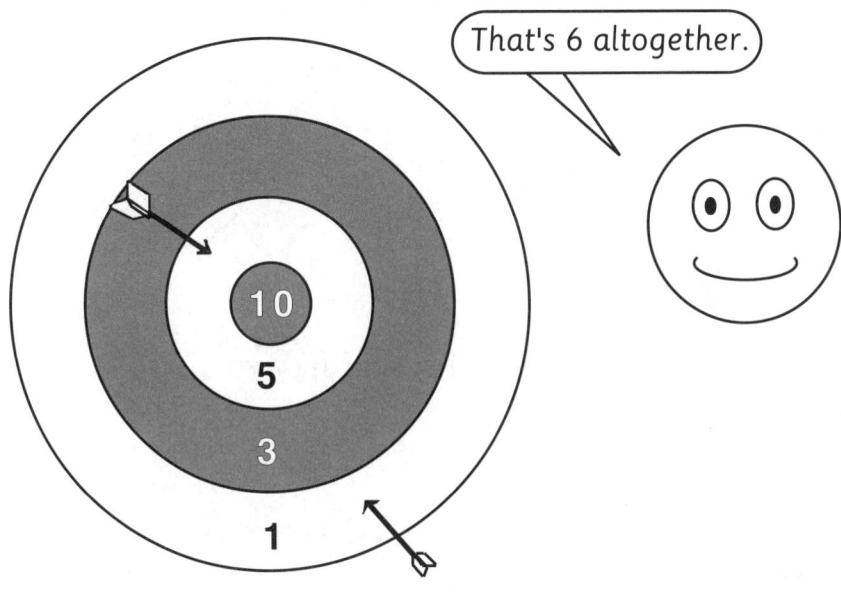

Max scored a ⑤ and a ①.

That's 6 altogether.

Minnie scored a ⑤ and ③.

That's ☐ altogether.

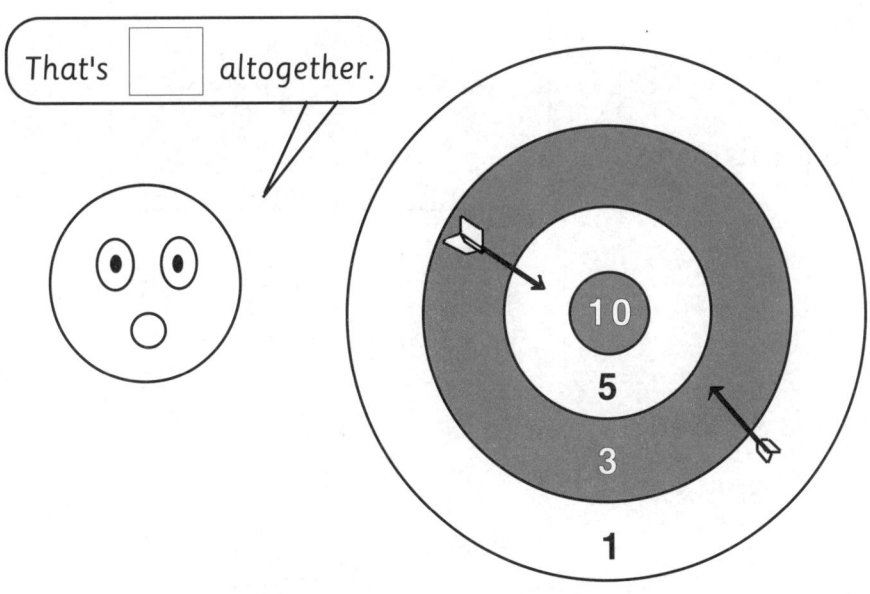

Who had the highest score?

_____ had the highest score.

How much more was Minnie's score than Max's?

Minnie's score was ☐ more.

Number Speed

Try to answer these questions as quickly as possible.

10 - 5 =

9 - 5 =

8 - 5 =

7 - 5 =

6 - 5 =

5 - 5 =

9 - 6 =

8 - 6 =

7 - 6 =

6 - 6 =

12 - 4 =

11 - 4 =

10 - 4 =

9 - 4 =

Fractions

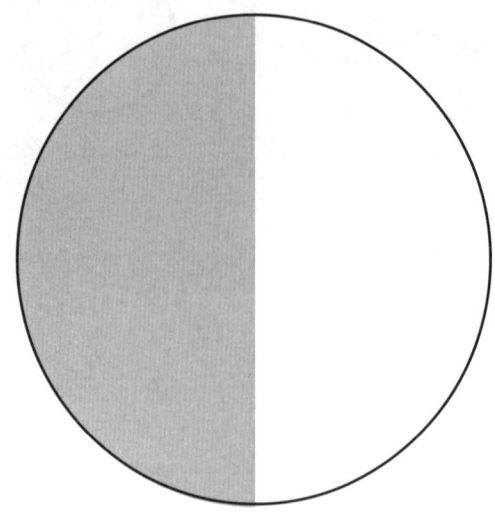

We can write half like this: $\frac{1}{2}$

We can write quarter like this: $\frac{1}{4}$

How much of each shape is shaded?

Write $\frac{1}{2}$ or $\frac{1}{4}$.

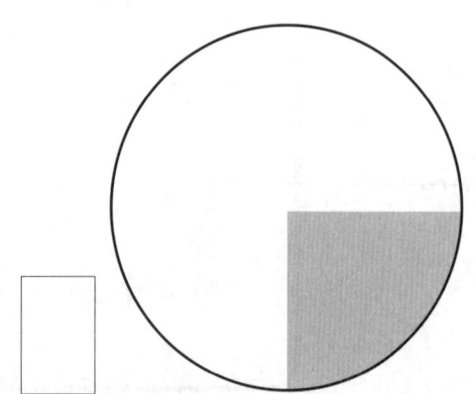

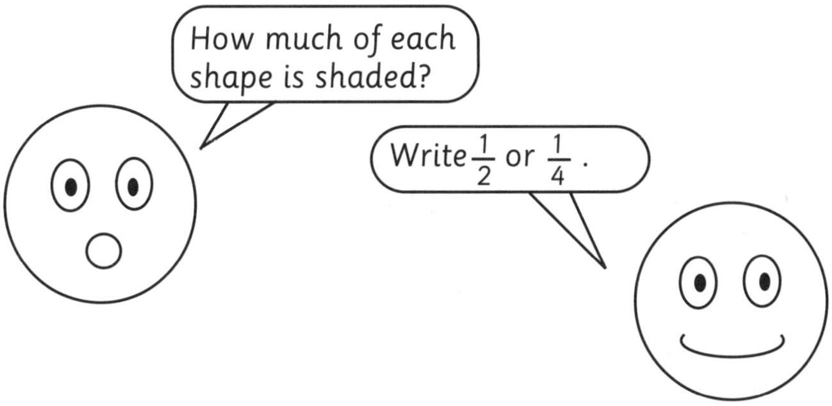

How much of each shape is shaded?

Write $\frac{1}{2}$ or $\frac{1}{4}$.

①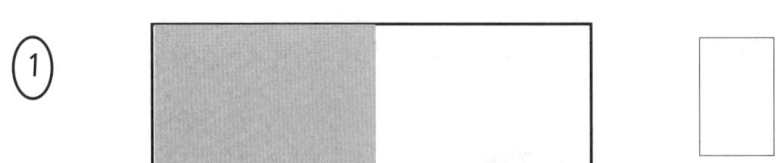

②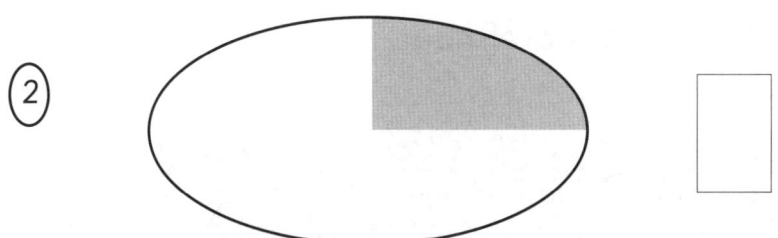

③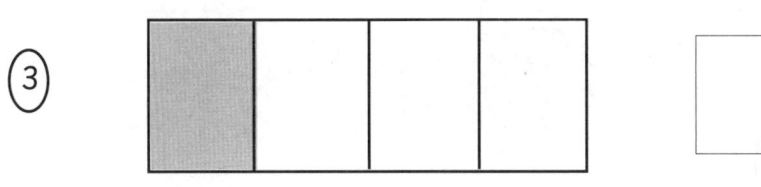

④

Number Speed

Try to answer these questions as quickly as possible.

$6 + 6 =$

$6 + 5 =$

$6 + 4 =$

$6 + 3 =$

$6 + 2 =$

$6 + 1 =$

$6 + 0 =$

$5 + 0 =$

$5 + 1 =$

$5 + 2 =$

$5 + 3 =$

$5 + 4 =$

$5 + 5 =$

$5 + 6 =$

$5 + 7 =$

More fractions

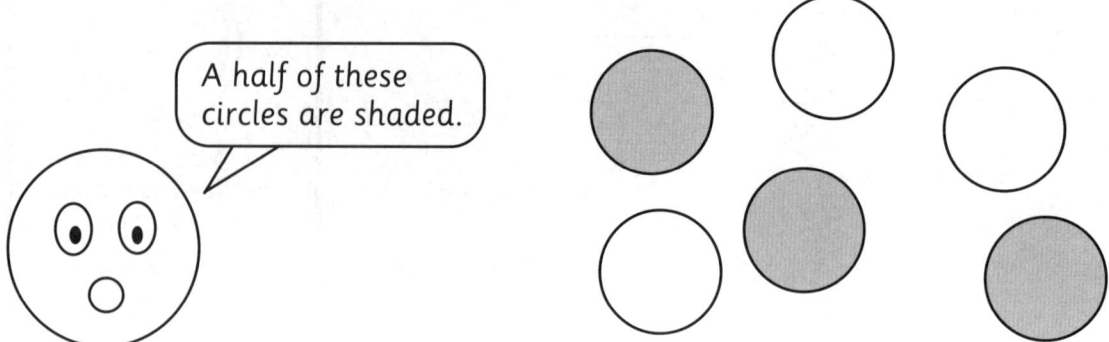

$\frac{1}{2}$ of all these circles are shaded.

$\frac{1}{2}$ of all these circles are not shaded.

In one of these sets, half of the circles are shaded.
Put a tick by the correct set.

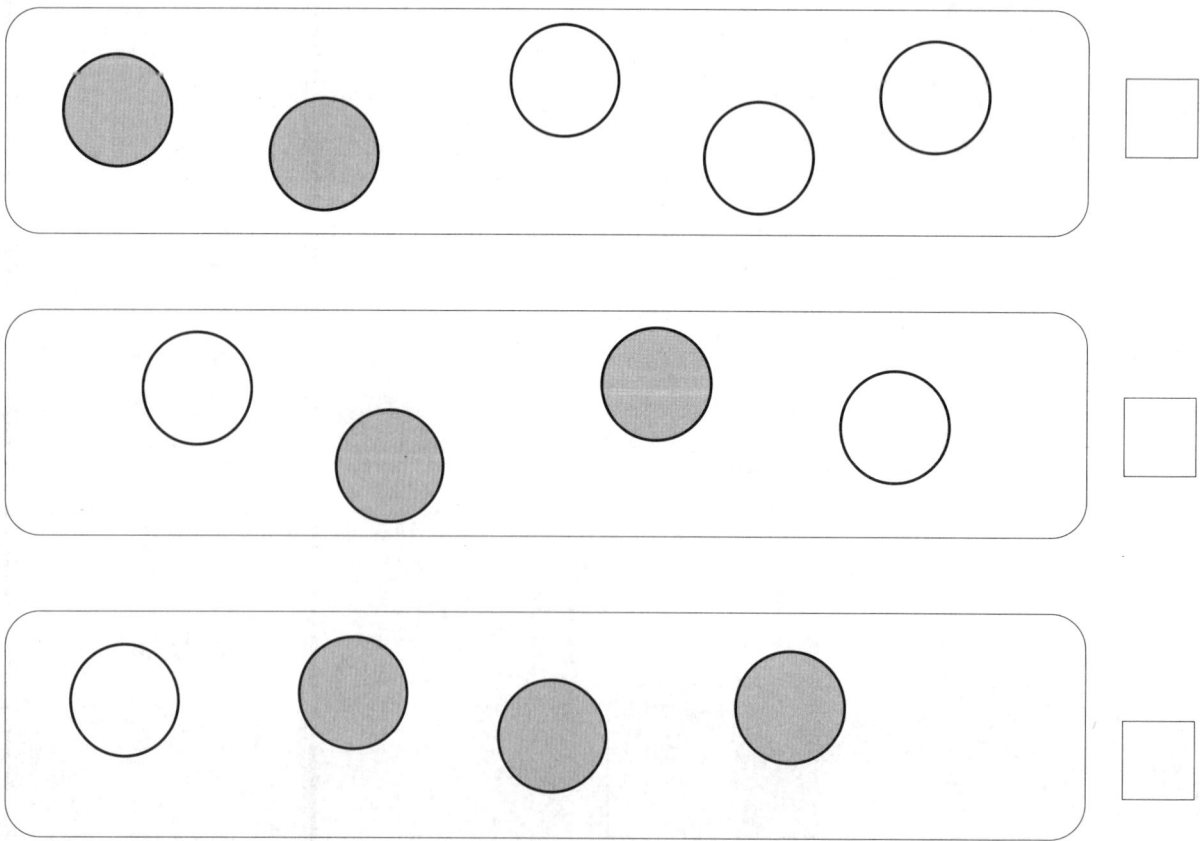

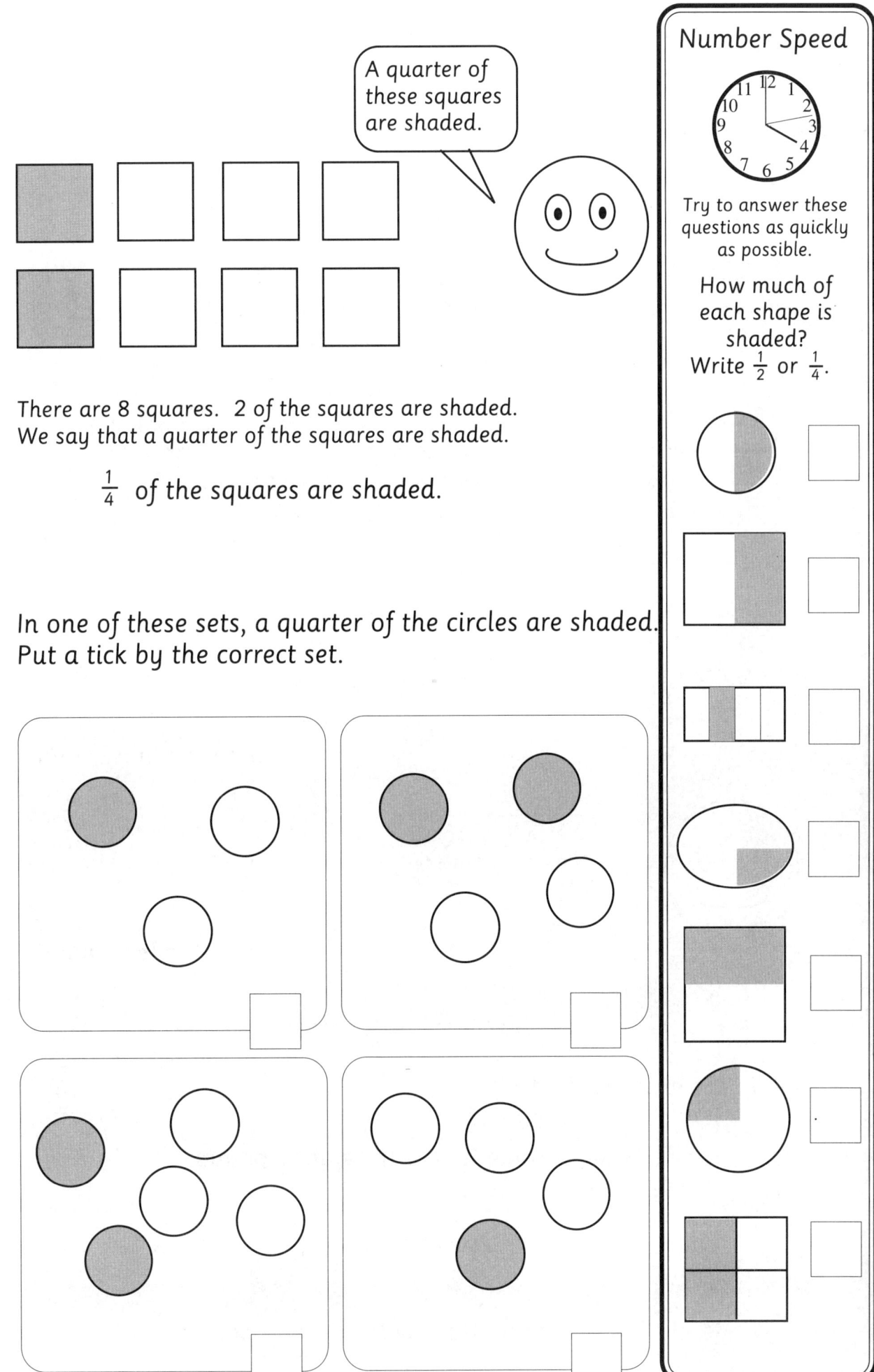

Most and Least

At a dog show the dogs were given points by the judges.

Fill in the missing words:

| Rex | came first with | eight | points. |

☐ came second with ☐ points.

☐ came third with ☐ points.

8 6 5 2

These numbers are in order from biggest to smallest.

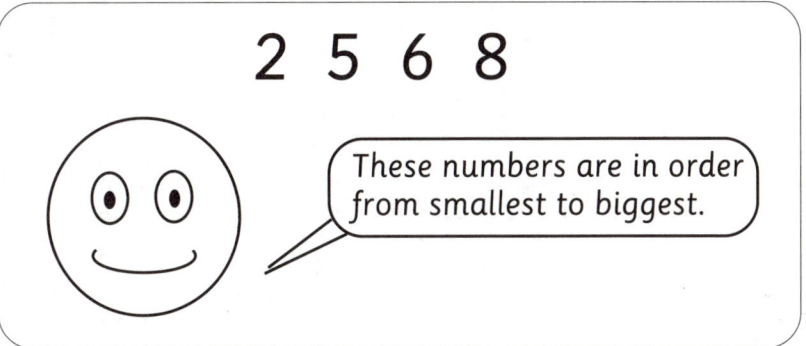

2 5 6 8

These numbers are in order from smallest to biggest.

Write these numbers in order, starting with the smallest:

9 6 4 7

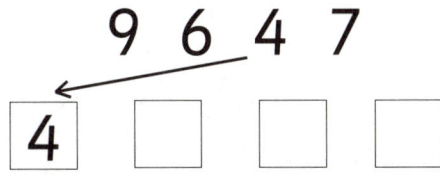

| 4 | | | |

Write these numbers in order, starting with the smallest:

3 8 4 2

10 6 1 12

20 10 40 30

15 5 25 10

Number Speed

Try to answer these questions as quickly as possible.

7 + 3 =

7 + 0 =

7 + 5 =

7 + 1 =

7 + 4 =

7 + 2 =

7 + 7 =

7 + 6 =

8 + 2 =

8 + 4 =

8 + 7 =

8 + 1 =

8 + 3 =

8 + 0 =

8 + 6 =

8 + 5 =

21

Multiplication

☆☆ One set of two stars. ⟶ 1 x 2 = 2

☆☆ ☆☆ Two sets of two stars. ⟶ 2 x 2 = 4

☆☆ ☆☆ ☆☆ ⟶ 3 x 2 = 6

☆☆ ☆☆ ☆☆ ☆☆ ⟶ 4 x 2 = 8

☆☆ ☆☆ ☆☆ ☆☆ ☆☆ ⟶ 5 x 2 = 10

☆☆ ☆☆ ☆☆ ☆☆ ☆☆ ☆☆ ⟶ 6 x 2 = 12

☆☆ ☆☆ ☆☆ ☆☆ ☆☆ ☆☆ ☆☆ ⟶ 7 x 2 = 14

☆☆ ☆☆ ☆☆ ☆☆ ☆☆ ☆☆ ☆☆ ☆☆ ⟶ 8 x 2 = 16

☆☆ ☆☆ ☆☆ ☆☆ ☆☆ ☆☆ ☆☆ ☆☆ ☆☆ ⟶ 9 x 2 = 18

☆☆ ☆☆ ☆☆ ☆☆ ☆☆ ☆☆ ☆☆ ☆☆ ☆☆ ☆☆ ▶ 10 x 2 = 20

The two times table

This is the two times table.
Fill in the missing answers.

1 x 2 =
2 x 2 =
3 x 2 =
4 x 2 =
5 x 2 =
6 x 2 =
7 x 2 =
8 x 2 =
9 x 2 =
10 x 2 =

You need to learn the multiplication tables.

Fill in the missing answers in these multiplication tables.
You can count on with your fingers to help you.

The three times table

1 x 3 = 3
2 x 3 = 6
3 x 3 = ☐
4 x 3 = 12
5 x 3 = ☐
6 x 3 = 18
7 x 3 = 21
8 x 3 = ☐
9 x 3 = 27
10 x 3 = ☐

The four times table

1 x 4 = 4
2 x 4 = ☐
3 x 4 = 12
4 x 4 = 16
5 x 4 = ☐
6 x 4 = 24
7 x 4 = ☐
8 x 4 = 32
9 x 4 = ☐
10 x 4 = 40

The five times table

1 x 5 = ☐
2 x 5 = 10
3 x 5 = ☐
4 x 5 = 20
5 x 5 = 25
6 x 5 = ☐
7 x 5 = 35
8 x 5 = ☐
9 x 5 = 45
10 x 5 = ☐

Number Speed

Try to answer these questions as quickly as possible.

6 x 2 =

4 x 3 =

3 x 4 =

1 x 4 =

2 x 2 =

5 x 3 =

7 x 2 =

5 x 5 =

2 x 4 =

3 x 5 =

4 x 5 =

3 x 2 =

9 x 2 =

4 x 4 =

2 x 3 =

0 x 4 =

23

Division

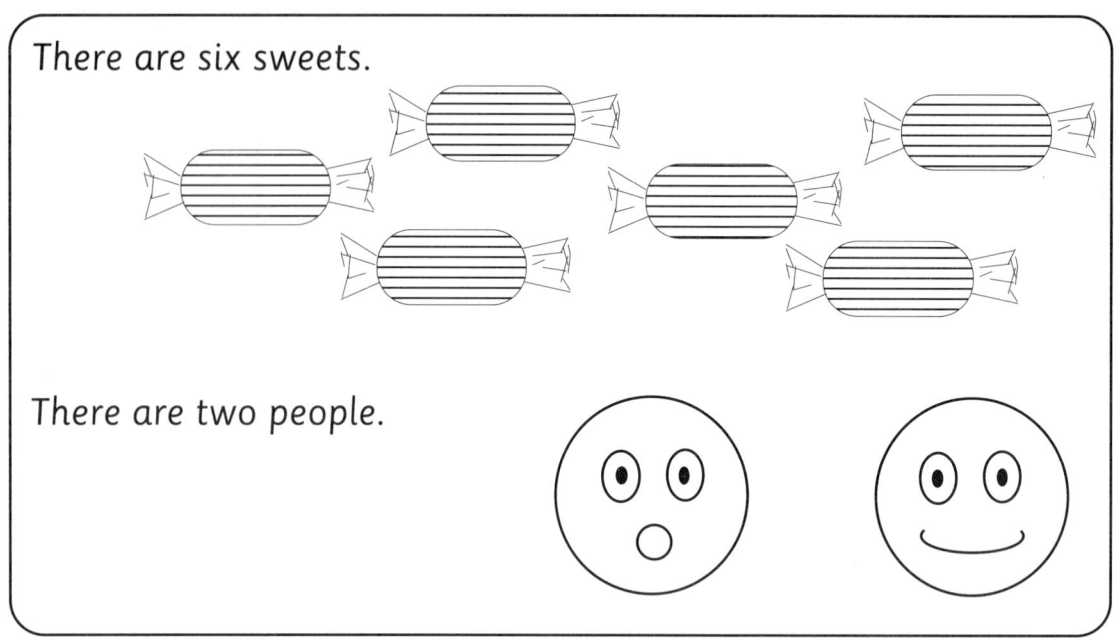

$$6 \div 2 = 3$$

Six divided by two is three.

2 x 3 = 6		2 x 4 = ☐		3 x 3 = ☐

3 x 2 = 6		4 x 2 = ☐		9 ÷ 3 = ☐

6 ÷ 2 = 3		8 ÷ 2 = ☐		2 x 2 = ☐

6 ÷ 3 = 2		8 ÷ 4 = ☐		4 ÷ 2 = ☐

4 x 4 = ☐   3 x 4 = ☐

16 ÷ 4 = ☐   4 x 3 = ☐

5 x 5 = ☐   12 ÷ 3 = ☐

25 ÷ 5 = ☐   12 ÷ 4 = ☐

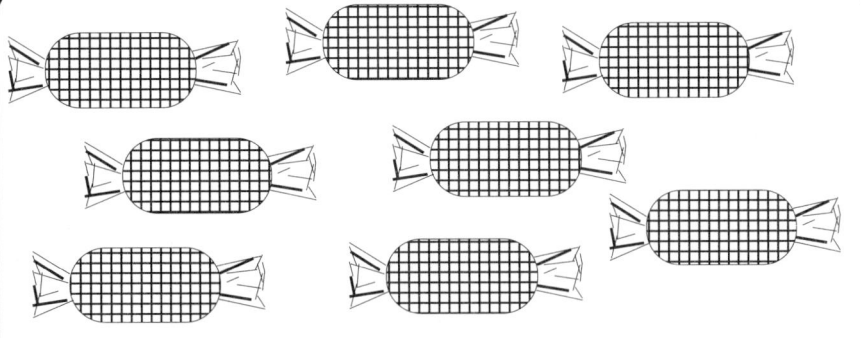

There are eight sweets.

How many sweets can we have each?

Max and Minnie can have ☐ sweets each.

5 x 2 = ☐   3 x 5 = ☐

2 x 5 = ☐   5 x 3 = ☐

10 ÷ 2 = ☐   15 ÷ 3 = ☐

10 ÷ 5 = ☐   15 ÷ 5 = ☐

Max and Minnie have 20p to share. How much can they have each? ☐

Number Speed

Try to answer these questions as quickly as possible.

6 ÷ 3 =

12 ÷ 4 =

15 ÷ 5 =

16 ÷ 4 =

8 ÷ 2 =

10 ÷ 2 =

12 ÷ 3 =

15 ÷ 3 =

4 ÷ 2 =

9 ÷ 3 =

8 ÷ 4 =

25 ÷ 5 =

20 ÷ 4 =

10 ÷ 5 =

30 ÷ 3 =

40 ÷ 4 =

Measurement

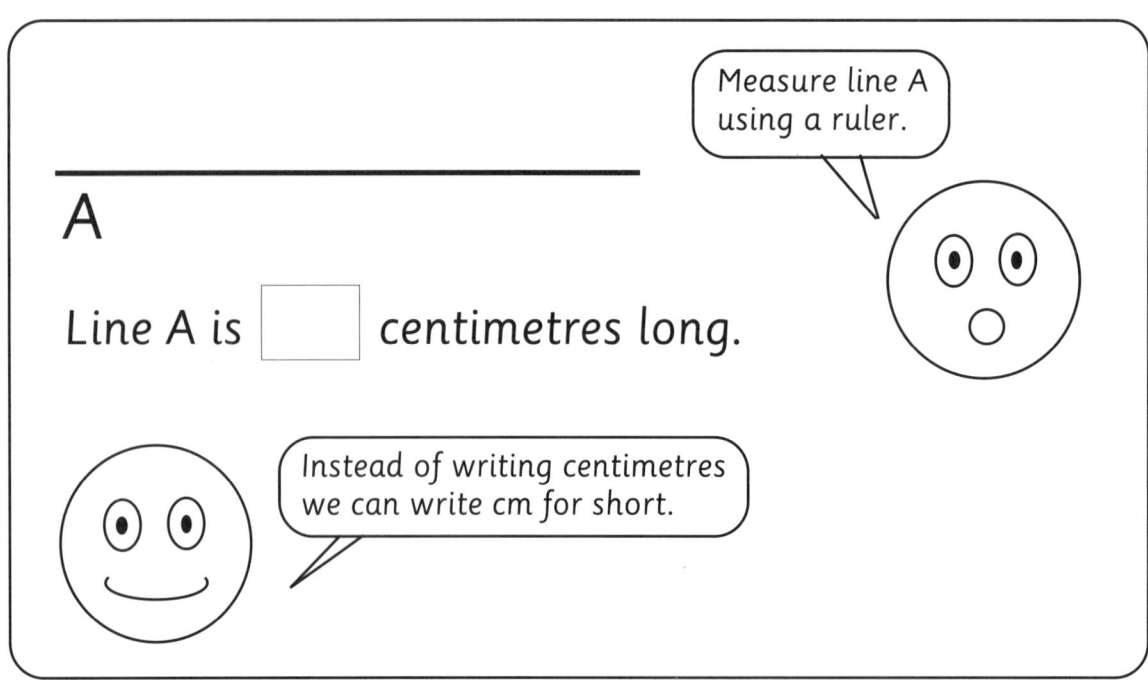

Measure these lines in centimetres:

B _____

Line B is ☐ cm long.

C _____

Line C is ☐ cm long.

D _____

Line D is ☐ long.

E _____

Line E is ☐ long.

F _____

Line F is ☐ long.

G _

Line G is ☐ long.

The longest line is line ☐ .　　The shortest line is line ☐ .

Numbers and words

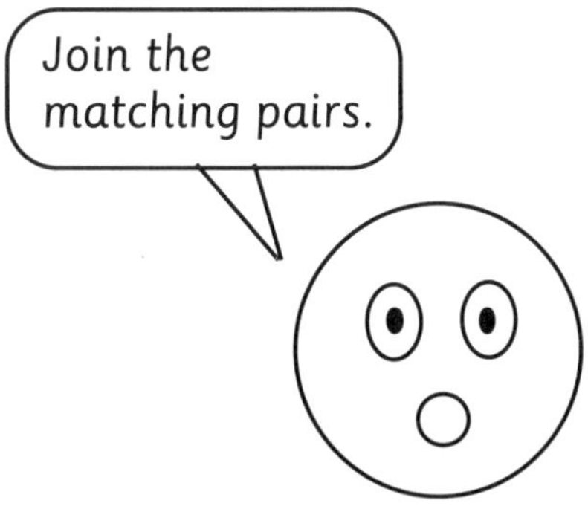

Join the matching pairs.

```
3  ——— twenty
7   \   three
15      seven
20      fifteen
```

twenty-one — 18
sixteen — 16
nine — 21
eighteen — 9

Write these numbers in figures:

eight → 8
five → ☐
ten → ☐
six → ☐
fourteen → ☐

four → ☐
twelve → ☐
seven → ☐
two → ☐
nine → ☐

Write the numbers in words:

16 → ☐
9 → ☐
17 → ☐
20 → ☐

Number Speed

Try to answer these questions as quickly as possible.

7 + 4 =

7 - 3 =

3 x 4 =

10 ÷ 2 =

5 + 5 =

6 - 4 =

5 x 4 =

12 ÷ 3 =

6 + 7 =

9 - 3 =

2 x 5 =

6 ÷ 3 =

8 + 4 =

12 - 7 =

5 x 5 =

9 ÷ 3 =

More addition

Draw a ring around the two numbers which add up to 8.

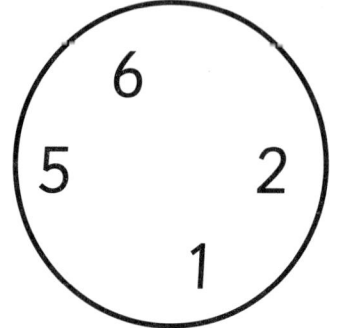

Draw a ring around the two numbers which add up to 6.

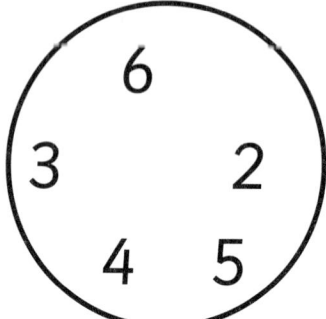

Draw a ring around the two numbers which add up to 9.

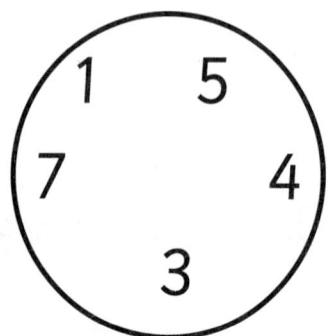

Draw a ring around the two numbers which add up to 10.

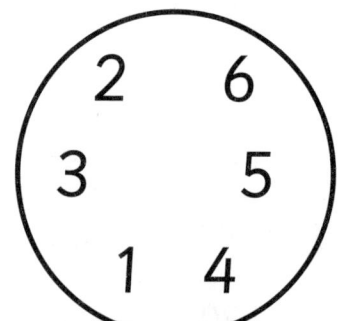

 Complete these additions.

```
  16        12        14
+  3      +  5      +  4
----      ----      ----

  11         8        13        15
+  3       + 7      +  3       +13
----      ----      ----      ----
```

 Complete these subtractions.

```
  17        14        13
-  9       - 6       - 7
----      ----      ----

  11        15        12        19
-  2       - 7       - 8       - 16
----      ----      ----      ----
```

If Max has 25p and Minnie has 12p, how much more has Max got than Minnie?

```
  25
- 12
----
```

Max has got ☐ p more than Minnie.

Number Speed

Try to answer these questions as quickly as possible.

10 + 3 =

10 + 13 =

10 + 23 =

10 + 33 =

12 + 5 =

12 + 15 =

12 + 25 =

12 + 35 =

6 + 9 =

16 + 9 =

26 + 9 =

36 + 9 =

46 + 9 =

56 + 9 =

29

More time

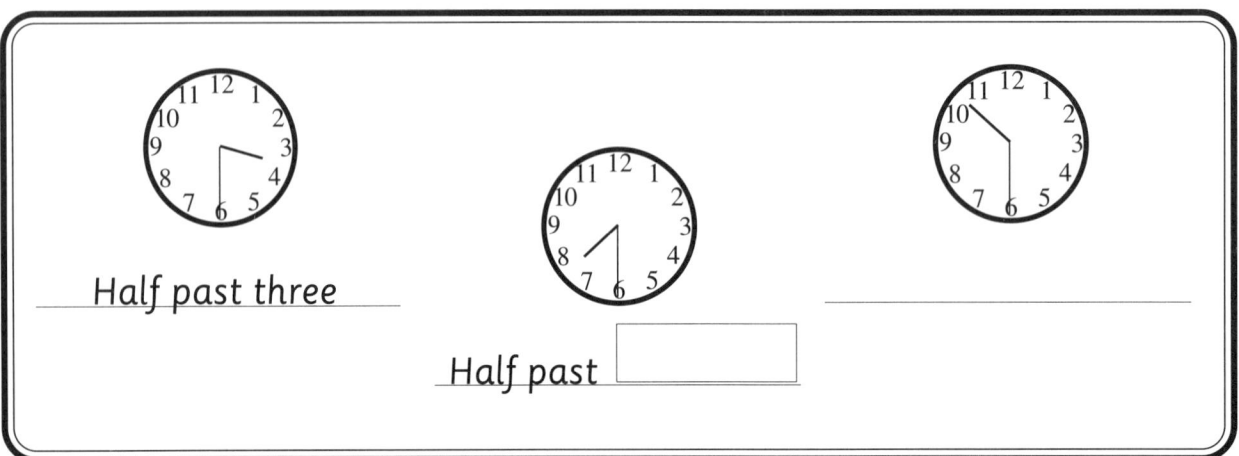

Half past three

Half past

Quarter past four

Draw lines to match the clock faces to the digital times.

05:15

08:15

02:15

09:30

01:15

08:30

11:15

Number Speed

Try to answer these questions as quickly as possible.

½ of 6 =

¼ of 8 =

½ of 10 =

½ of 12 =

¼ of 12 =

½ of 4 =

¼ of 4 =

½ of 2 =

¼ of 16 =

½ of 16 =

½ of 20 =

¼ of 20 =

½ of 18 =

½ of 14 =

½ of 100 =

Shopping

Apples 6p each

Bananas 8p each

Oranges 7p each

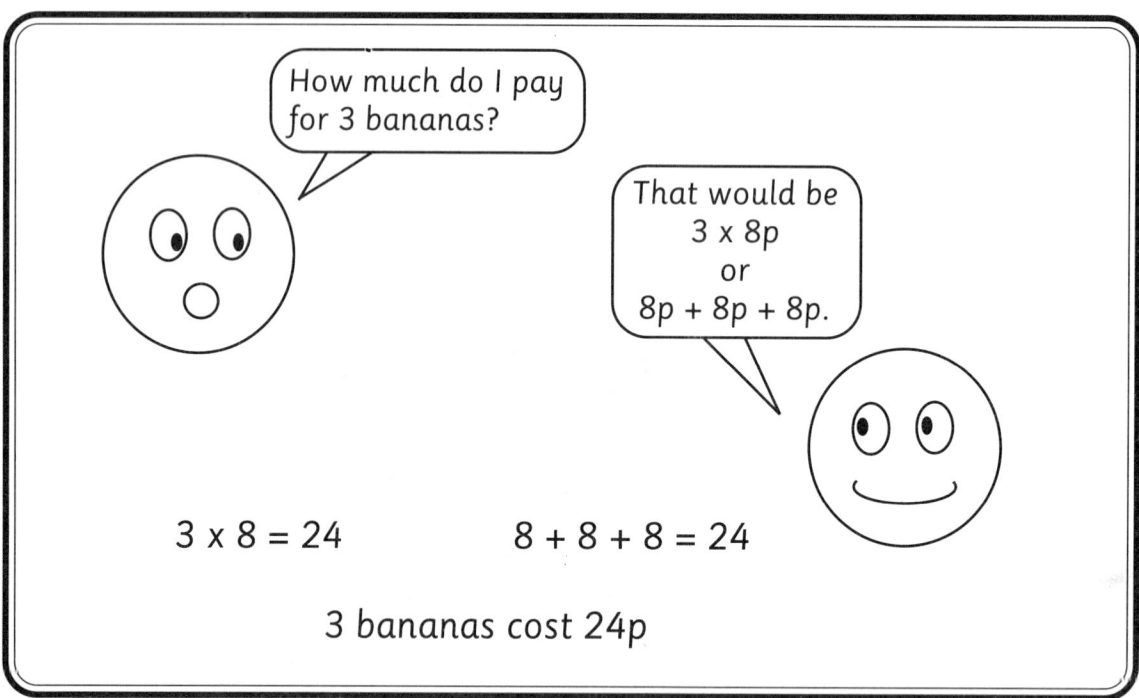

Work out these costs:

2 apples cost ☐ p   3 oranges cost ☐ p

2 bananas cost ☐ p   4 apples cost ☐ p

3 apples cost ☐ p   2 oranges cost ☐ p

3 apples and 2 oranges cost ☐ p altogether.

1 apple, 1 banana and 1 orange cost ☐ p altogether.

2 apples, 2 bananas and 2 oranges cost ☐ p altogether.

If I bought a banana and an apple how much change would I have from 20p?

A banana and an apple cost 14p altogether so the change from 20p is 6p.

Two oranges cost ☐ p.
　　　The change from 20p is ☐ p.

An apple and an orange cost ☐ p altogether.
　　　The change from 20p is ☐ p.

Two bananas and two oranges cost ☐ p altogether.
　　　The change from 50p is ☐ p.

One banana costs　　　　 p
Two apples cost　　　　　 p
Three oranges cost　　　　p
　　　　　　　　　　────
They cost　　　　　　　　p altogether.

The change from 50p is ☐ p.

Two bananas cost　　　　 p
One apple costs　　　　　 p
Two oranges cost　　　　 p
　　　　　　　　　　────
They cost　　　　　　　　p altogether.

The change from 50p is ☐ p.

Number Speed

Try to answer these questions as quickly as possible.

20 - 10 =

20 - 18 =

20 - 2 =

20 - 7 =

20 - 15 =

20 - 20 =

20 - 8 =

20 - 6 =

20 - 0 =

20 - 16 =

20 - 5 =

20 - 12 =

20 - 17 =

20 - 9 =

20 - 3 =

20 - 1 =

33

Graphs

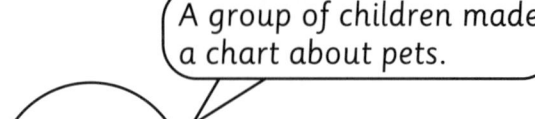 A group of children made a chart about pets.

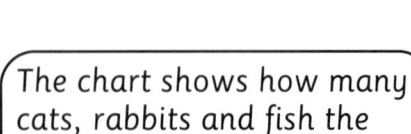 The chart shows how many cats, rabbits and fish the children had.

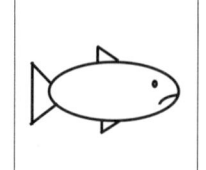
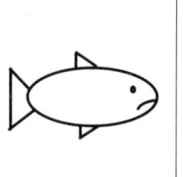
 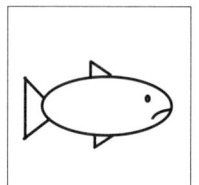
  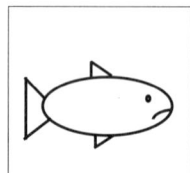

  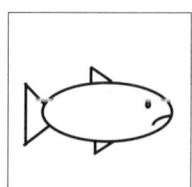

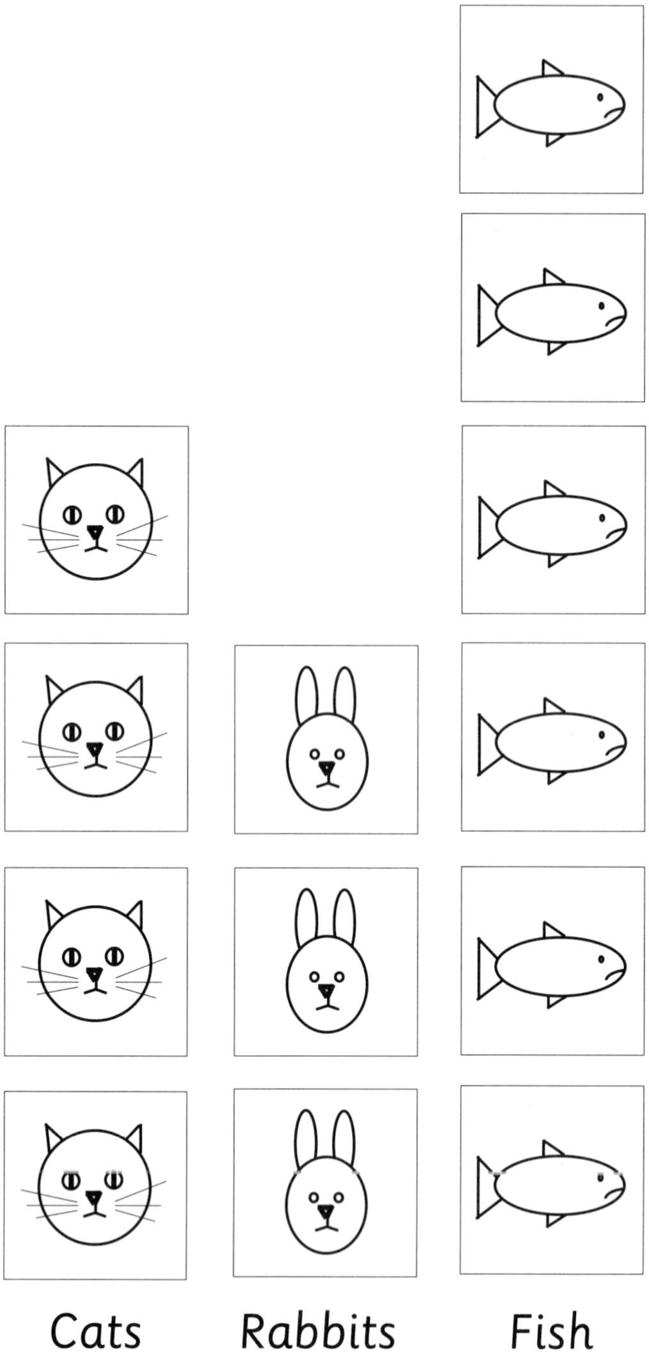

    Cats   Rabbits   Fish

Look at the chart to answer these questions:

    Which type of pet was the most popular?

    How many more cats than rabbits were there?

    How many more fish than cats?

    How many fewer rabbits than fish?

    How many pets were there altogether?

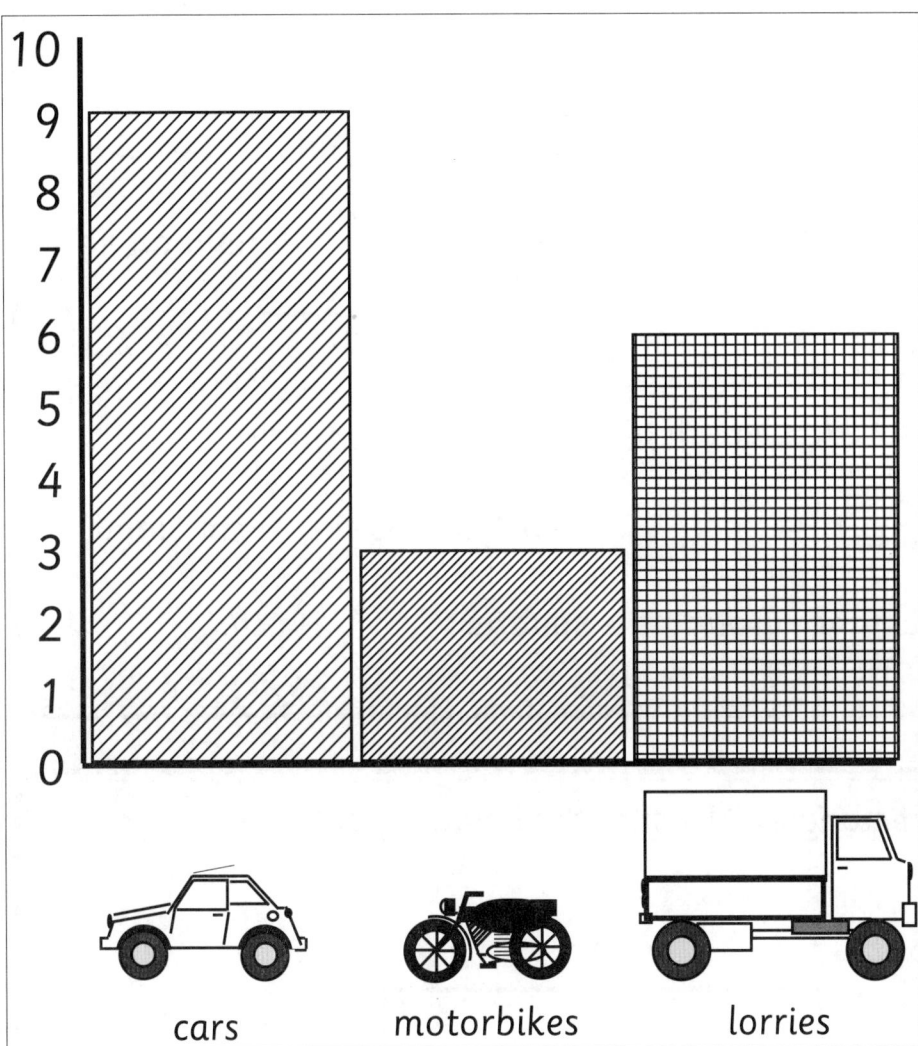

How many cars passed by? ☐

How many lorries passed by? ☐

How many motorbikes passed by? ☐

How many more cars than lorries passed by? ☐

How many fewer motorbikes than cars passed by? ☐

Number Speed

Try to answer these questions as quickly as possible.

1 x 2 =

2 x 2 =

3 x 2 =

4 x 2 =

5 x 2 =

1 x 3 =

2 x 3 =

3 x 3 =

4 x 3 =

5 x 3 =

1 x 4 =

2 x 4 =

3 x 4 =

4 x 4 =

5 x 4 =

0 x 3 =

Shapes

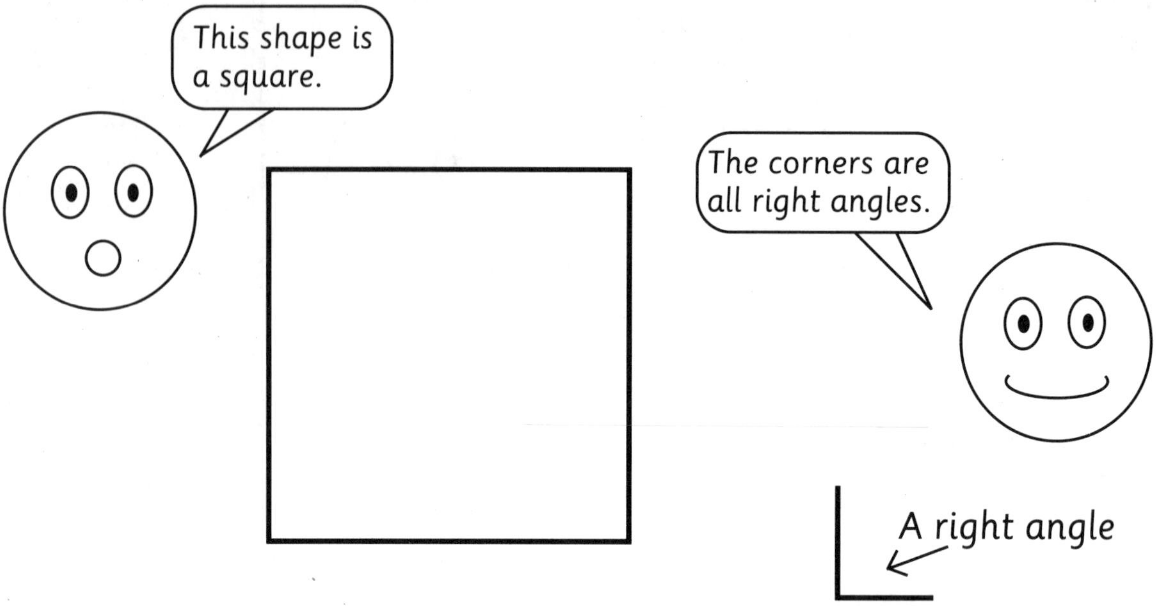

"This shape is a square."

"The corners are all right angles."

A right angle

Use a ruler to measure the length of each side of the square.

Each side is ☐ cm long.

What is the total distance around the square? ☐ cm

This shape is a rectangle. Measure the length of each side.

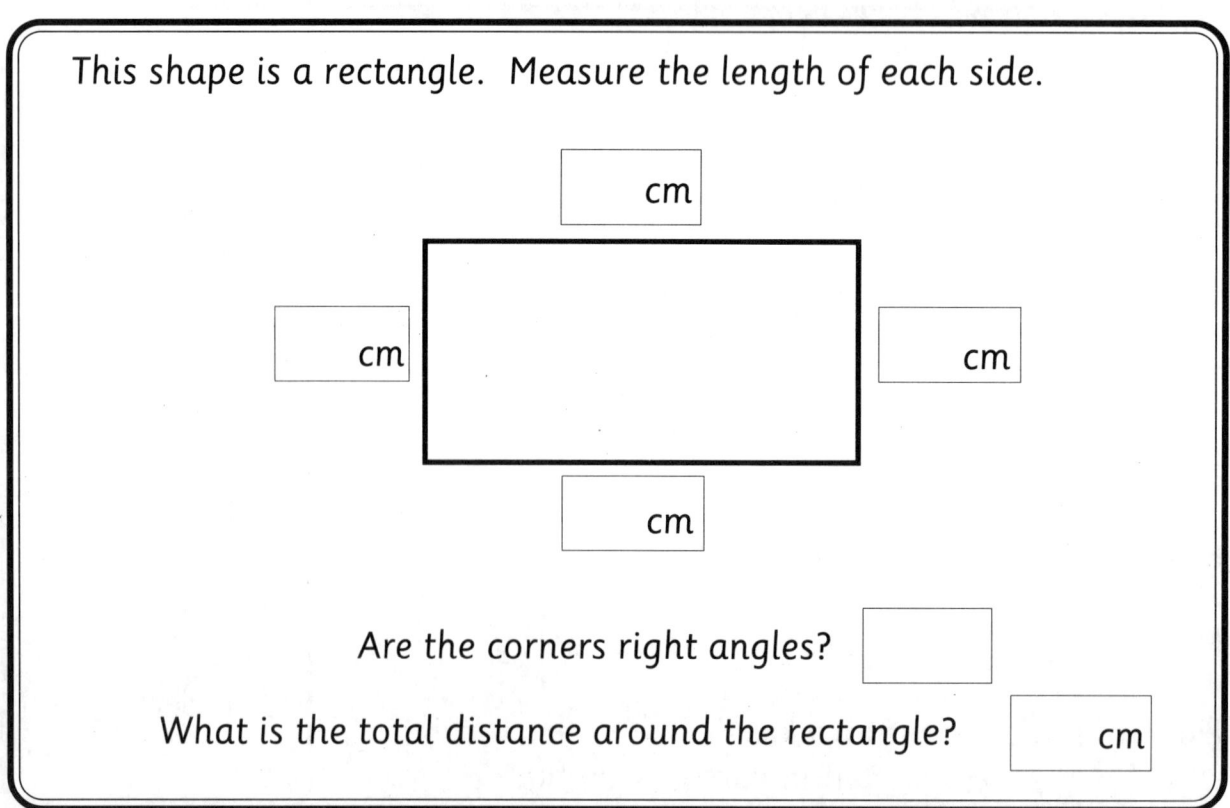

Are the corners right angles? ☐

What is the total distance around the rectangle? ☐ cm